Translated by Ardeth Neale

Mary the Life Saver

Louis-Philippe Hébert

BookLand press

Published by BookLand Press
15 Allstate Parkway, Suite 600
Markham, Ontario L3R 5B4
www.booklandpress.com

Printed in Canada

Front cover image © Melpomenem

Library and Archives Canada Cataloguing in Publication

Hébert, Louis-Philippe, 1946-
[Marie Réparatrice. English]
Mary the life saver / Louis-Philippe Hébert; Ardeth Neale, translator.

Translation of: Marie Réparatrice.
Poems.
Issued in print and electronic formats.
ISBN 978-1-77231-020-7 (paperback).--ISBN 978-1-77231-021-4 (epub).--
ISBN 978-1-77231-022-1 (pdf)

I. Title. II. Title: Marie Réparatrice. English.

PS8515.E2M3713 2015 C841'.54 C2015-907133-X
C2015-907134-8

Canada Council for the Arts Conseil des arts du Canada
ONTARIO ARTS COUNCIL
CONSEIL DES ARTS DE L'ONTARIO
an Ontario government agency
un organisme du gouvernement de l'Ontario
Société de développement des entreprises culturelles
Québec

We acknowledge the support of the Canada Council for the Arts, which last year invested $157 million to bring the arts to Canadians throughout the country. We acknowledge the support of the Ontario Arts Council (OAC), an agency of the Government of Ontario. Translation of this book was generously supported by the Société de développement des entreprises culturelles du Québec (SODEC).

To my daughters

This morning I saved the life of a cat
it wasn't so hard to do
the cat just lay there
he was all limp

accidents can happen so quickly
the street was deserted
the car didn't stop
it just kept on going
cars don't stop for cats
for dogs neither
cars are too busy to bother
with cats that get crushed

a cat is pretty fixable
but you need all the parts
I carried him to the sidewalk
I'd cried cat! look out!
but the car didn't listen

when I took him up in my arms
I noticed the cat had drool on his maw
that's what it's called
a maw, I know

cuz when my father says
shut your maw
my mom always answers
maw is for animals

for humans we say mouth
it's not a big deal
it's just words
maw is good for cats

cats don't talk
they meow
this cat didn't meow
he had his eyes open
there is no special word
for the eyes of a cat
even if they were dead
and didn't move

eyes are just eyes
eyes work for humans
just like for animals
even flies have eyes
an eye isn't like a maw
mine is a mouth
my father says
mine is a pretty little maw
I don't think that's nice

I have two eyes
my eyes are so good
that my mom often says
your eyes are sharp like a cat's
you don't need to wear glasses
so I could even lose one
I've got two
that wouldn't be so bad
you can still see with one eye
when you've got sharp eyes like a cat

I scooped up the poor cat into my arms
he wasn't moving
he didn't try to get away
like cats do
when you pick them up
and try to cuddle them
and they didn't think of it first

that cat was a mess
his fur was all mucky
with blood and dirt
and saliva
I know that we say drool
when it comes from a cat
saliva is for humans

he wasn't moving
he wasn't breathing
there was no beating inside
if the heart was beating
I would have seen it
cuz his tummy was split open
there was stuff coming out
stuff I'd never seen before
stuff I have no name for

my name is Mary
I have a name
and my name is Mary
when my mom calls out Mary
I say
Mom I'm here

when I'm older it's going to be
Sister Mary
Mary Reparatrix

Sister Mary Reparatrix
cuz I'm going to be a nun
for real
once on TV there was a nun
she was a Reparatrix nun
they repair the world
just like I do
the nun said when Heaven blesses you
with a special gift
you must be grateful
you must use your gift with care

I know what she means
even if I'm only eight and a half
I live in a world
where lots of accidents happen
luckily I was given a special gift

when I'm older
I'll enter a convent
to be protected
from everything bad
cuz I'm Heaven blessed
cuz I am grateful too of course
but that's not for yet
my father won't hear of it
not for a second
he says not a chance
that's all there is to it

that is just foolishness Mary
my father calls me Mary when he wants to scold me
usually he calls me kitty cat
I hate it when he calls me that

the cat is Eugenya
you have to say you-gee-nyah
that's my cat
she was so brave
she didn't cry
the whole time
my cat's no scaredy cat
she kept her eyes wide open
even while she was dead

it all happened so quickly
my cat probably didn't even see
the car
didn't brake
my mom always says
it's dangerous to cross the street
without looking
especially don't run
the cat was running
my cat didn't even scream
there was just a weird sound
it was like something fell into water
it was a strange kind of sound
that's what made me think the worst

the houses around didn't budge
no people rushed out
they were glued to their TVs
or else having supper
cuz it was suppertime
and my father hadn't come home yet

there is a space between our house
and the neighbour's house
not too wide
just some grass and a pathway
that leads to the backyard
where there's a raised swimming pool

I carried the cat there
as well as I could
which means not very well
I had to stop often
so I wouldn't lose any parts

inside parts
I don't know what they're called
kept spilling out onto the lawn
things belonging to our cat
Eugenya
I know it's a funny name
for a cat
Eugenya
you have to say you-gee-nyah

she was our cat
and even if it sounded funny
I kept on calling out
Euge-nya Euge-nya
she didn’t answer
she never did
in any case
our cat never obeyed
anyhow cats
never do

my father sometimes says
I’m as stubborn as a cat
when I do as I please
my father gets mad
when I don’t obey

Eugenya our cat
loved to hunt
when she’d see a bird
she would start chomping at the air
her paws would twitch
her claws would go in and out
it seemed like she wanted to jump
right through the window pane

we would open the door
and she would run across the street
without looking left or right
she'd cross without looking
cats aren't like children
they never obey
there is no use getting mad at them
cats don't understand
they don't care

in the park across the street
she'd catch squirrels
she was always in such a hurry to get to the park
that's why she ran
across the street without looking

my mom says always look both ways
before crossing the street
she even predicted it
she said one of these days
with the cat running out like he does
an accident is sure to happen

my mom knows things I don't know
she knows what is coming
what is gone she says
is best to forget

one of these days he's going to get hit
sometimes we say he when we talk about Eugenya
but we're supposed to say she
cuz it was only later
after we baptized the cat Eugene
that we found out
too late
obviously
that he was a she-cat
so we just added a nyah sound
now it's Eugenya
like nyah nyah it's not a big mistake
so there now
our cat has a girl's name

my father says to use female
when talking about animals
we should say female
woman and girl are only for humans
not for animals
for humans it's different

so why does my dad
when he's upset with my mom or me
and he's yelling at us
call us the females of the house
he's making a mistake

my mom says that my dad
makes many mistakes
he makes mistakes but he's not bad
he's just tired

at times he thinks the females of the house
are in league against him
he says even the cat
is on mom's side just like me
my mother says we have to be careful
of the words that we choose
cuz words can hurt feelings

words like cow
a cow looks pretty a in a field
not in a house

people say I think about too many things
at the same time
and they are right
but I always remember
what I'm saying and thinking
and Eugenya no matter what happens
I'll never forget you

after the accident everything went quiet and still
it seemed like there was just me and the cat
when I picked up Eugenya
from the asphalt
when I carried my cat
from the middle of the street
to the sidewalk
I said over and over Eugenya my love
my sweet pussycat
just like my father says to my mom
when he's in a good mood
and he whispers to her sweet nothings
and calls her pet names
not names like fat cow
that's never nice

since Eugenya didn't answer me
I carried her to the backyard
my darling Eugenya
and placed her in the shade
of the pool on the grass
I sprinkled pool water onto the head of my cat
and sewed her up
my sweet Eugenya
I put her back together
with my fingers
you can just pretend you know
it is still going to work

I told myself
no need for a needle and thread
I just pushed in what was out
and sewed her all up

then I just did like I do
when I want something to work
I concentrated real hard
like when you try to open a door
and it's locked
but you don't know that it's locked
well for me the door opens

I placed my hand on her head
between those small pointy ears
I focused really hard
and her eyes opened
this wasn't pretend magic
this was real
there was no trick
that you find out about later
like those magic tricks
done with two-way mirrors
where they can see through one side
or with cards that are nicked
so that they can cheat
it's not nice to cheat
me I don't cheat
never

after she was mended
Eugenya looked up at me
as if she was seeing me
for the very first time with those eyes
they was so bright
I have to stop saying they was
it's they were I know it
then she took off running

I know that by doing that
I mean repairing live things
saving animals and insects
especially after a big accident like that one
I knew it might cost me a lot
I could become blind for example
but I like it so much
that look that they give me
when they come back to life
when it works
this little miracle of mine
my gift
I've got two anyhow
eyes two sharp eyes I could always lose one
and still be able to see

it's just that I can't
lose them both

it was with my guinea pig that I figured out my gift
and the price that it costs me
my guinea pig
but that's a whole other story
a story that begins with a moth
a story always has a beginning
and an end you'll see

first I have to tell you about the moth
nighttime butterfly I say
that's prettier than moth
if you want to understand
I have no idea how it got
into my bedroom
or why it wouldn't move
it was very pretty
it was the color and shape of a leaf
but it wasn't a leaf
I could see that right away
I've got sharp eyes

its wings looked kind of broken
it stayed there stuck to the wall
even when I cried fly
fly away
out you go shoo
or else my father will get mad
he's going to kill you

the butterfly just stayed there
all day without moving
so that night after supper I placed it onto my fingertip
again I told it fly away
I'm telling you for the last time
so then I concentrated
and I done it
it worked

I can't say
that it cost me so much
I only lost a fingernail
the butterfly was less damaged
than my guinea pig
or maybe when it's a less
complicated form of life
it's not as hard to repair must be
cuz that time it was easy

my nail went all black
there is always a price to pay
my father says you should pay your debts
right on the nail
well mine turned black
and fell off

but my guinea pig
it died of poison
that's what my mom said
she said that the guinea pig stayed awake all night
it would make so much noise
running round on the wheel
the squeaky noise kept my father awake
my dad is a light sleeper must be
cuz the cage is beside my bed
and I never heard a thing

so then my guinea pig
must have eaten something bad
I heard that scientists use guinea pigs
for their experiments
cuz a guinea pig body
is a like a human body
only smaller

my guinea pig was dead
but it looked fast asleep
on its back face up to the sky
its cute little paws all curled in
so I did what I did
with the nighttime butterfly
and I done it
it worked

I held my guinea pig speaking softly
I put my fingers on its tummy
its paws twitched
the very next day I got a broken arm

my father thinks that
it will cost an arm and a leg
when I tell him I want something
and he asks why I want it
I just say that I need it
my eye you do
an arm and a leg
my father says that
it's one of his favourite expressions
I was beginning to get what he means
cuz it happened to me for real
but my guinea pig was happy
to still be alive
and me too

for a cat it's different
a cat is more complicated
it loves more
everyone knows that
a cat can understand more
it's more intelligent
you don't get nothin for nothin

that's what my father taught me
so when I give somethin
I have to lose somethin
that's just the price I have to pay

I saw it first with my fingernail
when it turned black
and then fell off
Mom took a fit
how on earth did that happen
we rushed to the hospital
and ran in
we hurried to Emergency
but we got stuck there waiting
for nothin
Mom's face was all tight
she was worried
for nothin I say
the doctor told her
there's nothing to worry about
your daughter must have hit it
with a hammer or a rock
or in a door got it caught

but no Mom no
why does he say that
I know what happened
It's not like he says

I just put a nighttime butterfly
onto my nail
you mean a moth
and I brought it back to life

that's impossible don't be silly
that's what my mom said

but it's true Mom
it's just like with food
you have to eat to stay alive
you say so yourself Mom
so that we can eat
some animal must suffer

just don't talk like that
in front of your father

my father is a butcher
he says I talk as if I'm a vegetarian
but I know how real life works

I too have to suffer
and I sacrifice a part of myself
just like a calf
he suffers too
the calf
when he gives us his liver

so that we can stay alive
the calf gives us calf liver
he makes sacrifices
him too

stop this silly nonsense right now

but Mom I am
like the calf and his calf liver
I gave a fingernail I'd give an arm
so that another could live
that's my special gift

but that's impossible my little lamb
Mom said it over and over
I think she must have been talking to herself

she placed her finger onto my lips
just like I did with the butterfly
onto my fingertip
and she made me feel so much better
it felt to me like my lips
were the butterfly's wings
I gave my mom's finger a gentle kiss
and I thought of the fluttering wings
never mind all that
your nail will grow again
that's what my mom said

I didn't say anything
I could have said
no Mom I know it won't grow
I had to give up my fingernail
it was for the butterfly
when I brought it back to life
so my nail won't grow again
because what I give
I don't take back
cuz when you give something
and then take it back
that's like stealing

my mom was saying hush
I said nothing more
not a word
for one whole minute
which is pretty rare
for me

what's given is given
no take backs that's stealin
the same goes for my arm
I was talking to myself
but did not argue
I know it's a lost cause
the fracture won't heal
the bone isn't repairable

what's this all about
my father asked at suppertime
when he saw my arm in a cast
are you crazy or what

sometimes there is no use explaining
when someone doesn't understand
he just doesn't understand
my father wasn't interested in knowing
what really happened
he was furious
that my guinea pig
had come back to life
and would keep him awake again
every night

I already knew it would cost me an arm
no need to look at the cost of a bike
just cuz my bike was in pretty bad shape
no need to have a fit like a madman

it's true my bike was a wreck though

I'm not worried
I have another one
not a bike an arm
when I'm hungry my grandma says
well then eat up your left arm

and save the other for tomorrow
she's funny when she says that
but losing an arm
isn't funny at all

cuz to play dodge ball
you can't play as well
with only one arm

I had watched the doctor
stitching my arm
I looked real closely
at how he sewed my skin
but for a cat
with its fur and all its inside stuff
I had no idea how
I was supposed to do it

so I just pretended to sew up the cat
but still I knew
it would cost me for real
if not my sight then one eye for sure
cuz that cat is the apple of my eye
and cuz a cat
it's more complicated
I have to give more
for the gift to work

the cat seems in pretty good shape now
but my eye really itches
and everyone knows
you can't scratch an eye

Eugenya ran back to the park
top speed
to catch those squirrels
but she never eats them
she only catches them
without hurting or biting
still the squirrels don't like
being trapped in a cat's mouth
a cat's maw I know! I know!
no need to repeat it
I got it the first time

she seemed faster than before
maybe I had given too much
of my energy
to the cat
I guess tonight at supper
my father will scold me
for slouching
at the table
he'll say that it's my own fault
if I have this ugly sty
it's because I keep scratching it
with my dirty fingers

just look at those nails
you have to be crazy to behave like you do
he's going to start shouting
I work day in and day out
and look at you both
you don't lift a finger for me

my mother will answer
stop getting so worked up
I work as well
and Mary gets good marks at school
it's only an allergy
we should get rid of the cat
there that's what we should do

I screamed no
no never
after all that I've given up of myself
so that he can still be here

we should also get rid of that guinea pig
that makes such a racket at night
and keeps everyone awake
even the neighbours

that's not true that's not true

it seemed like he wanted to shake me
he could see very well that I still had my cast
and that my arm was broken
in a few places
and it still wasn't mended

look at her eye for Pete's sake
how does she do all this to herself
she's your daughter
so you tell me
and since when does she have allergies

my father had to wonder
it's only normal
when I had broken my arm
he wouldn't stop talking in the car
on our way back from the hospital
did you see how she broke it
Mary hurt herself riding her bike
and the bike is damaged too
but he wouldn't stop there
he was complaining about everything
me I was just an excuse
lots of things bugged him
besides my arm and my banged-up bike

thing weren't going well at work
at home neither

my mom and his boss
he says they're the same
those two are never satisfied
they never understand a thing

he was at the end of his rope
my mother said change jobs then
where do you want me to go
money doesn't grow on trees
my mom said
it's another economic meltdown
my father thought
she was making fun of him
that she was saying
that he was having a meltdown
an economic meltdown
that she was laughing at him for talking about money
that she was being ironic
just like we learn about in English class
my father got so angry
he started to sulk
that stopped his complaining
at least that counts for something

that time it was tough
I don't regret it though
my guinea pig is my friend

and I couldn't let my friend die
especially not
before we gave it a name

we didn't have a name for the guinea pig yet
we didn't want to make the same mistake
as we did with the he-cat
who was really a she-cat
we waited so we could be sure
but then we forgot
this is why my guinea pig wasn't baptized
I couldn't possibly let it go to Heaven
unbaptized
not knowing its own name

like at the Gate what's your name
and you have to answer just Whatsit
I admit for the butterfly
I didn't know its name neither
but you can't just sit and do nothin
I had to start somewhere
so I started with something small

besides we have ten fingernails
twenty if we count our toes
I can't believe some little kids call them
feet fingers but anyhow
that still makes twenty

so *losing* just one is a small price to pay
for a pretty nighttime butterfly moth
in life you have to make sacrifices
that's what my dad says

my black fingernail fell off
my father didn't say anything
if he imagined I had a gift
it would have been for woodworking
cuz he gave me a tool box
with a hammer and a saw
he might have wanted to give me a butcher's kit
but with a fingernail missing
I'm sure that he doubted
I had any talents at all

really now
that eye is as red as a tomato
my father wasn't pleased
he's my dad
I wasn't going to start lecturing him
about the cost of living
the way my mom tends to do
her two cents worth he says

I could have explained about the sentimental value
that is what costs me a lot
when I do a good deed
or one not so good

especially since the cat
they could do without
cuz of the allergies he gives
and the guinea pig too
but they couldn't really just sit there
and do nothin
about me

my father got in the car
which was parked in the garage
when he saw the cat
that wanted to sit on my lap
jump up on me
while he was trying
to buckle me in
cuz I couldn't see nothin
with just one eye
and also it's dark in that garage
I just couldn't do it
with my arm in a cast
he started to shout
oh not that cat again
can't we have some peace
for once in a while
Eugenya was purring
she was being all affectionate
she knew
that I just needed to be loved

damn cat
my father grabbed her by the scruff
and threw her
out of the car
Holy Moly!
the cat scrammed
I knew I'd go blind
if I tried to save her
the second time

just try to explain what you did
after that
you'd better keep quiet
Miss Mary Reparatrix
even to the doctor you just pretended
to the doctor you said
it was because you were on your bike
that you tried to jump
over the curb
and it didn't work
cuz your bike didn't want to
you didn't dare mention
the ones you had saved
that you know there's a cost
it could be an arm or an eye
cuz when you love
there is always a price to pay

the doctor had a plug
in his ear
that means he is deaf
except
when Daddy raised his voice
the doctor said
no need to shout I'm not deaf

and you think about this in the car
all the way home
the children he's healed
your arm in a cast
your ointment soaked eye patch
the black nail that fell off
so you think you're in pretty bad shape Miss Mary
you say it's normal to suffer
that you can't give somethin
without losing somethin else
well that doctor lost his hearing
by healing children
so you and your little hurts they're nothin
nothin at all
compared to that
so you have nothin to brag about my kitty
cuz when it's all over the pain is gone
it doesn't hurt anymore OK

and Mary you're not even hungry
so even if you went to bed
without supper
what difference would it make

I'm going to bed
without supper
yes I'm not hungry

look she's even lost her appetite
when did that start
this is your fault
you should look after her better
during all that
Eugenya managed to get into the house
I know her hiding place
near the door to the garage

I lay on my bed
on top of the covers
Eugenya came and snuggled next to me
the guinea pig too
even though you're not supposed to let it out of the cage
if you don't want it to swallow
every little thing that it finds

I am really not allowed
to sleep with my pets
but that night I didn't care
besides Eugenya had never ever hurt
my friend with no name my guinea pig
that for now we call Whatsit
she knows it's not an overgrown squirrel
my cat can tell the difference
she knows it's just like a person
that they use them in experiments
I saw so on the internet
sometimes it's not a pretty sight

my little darlings were cuddled
against the curve of my legs
as though our bodies were piled
one on top of the other
but sideways

I have no idea if there's a special word
for the bodies of animals
maybe it is carcass
that's such an ugly word
that's the word they use
in the butcher shop
where my father works
that's what I've heard them say
the one-eyed me
with an arm in a cast
I can still hear fine

I'm not deaf you know
I've still got both my ears
and the cat hasn't got my tongue yet

on Google I read that it's called carrion
that's for an animal that is dead
and it really stinks
carrion is creepy
my father says carrion
to swear
when he is angry
and that the head butcher is that
carrion
cuz he leaves him only the small pieces
to chop
what carrion his boss is too
cuz the boss refuses to understand
that my father wants a raise
it's like with my mom
the whole world is against him

I could hear them last night
my dad and my mom
it was after I had pretended
to swallow my pills
the ones for my allergies

and I had closed my door
I could hear them
cuz I have sharp hearing like a cat
not just the eyes
like my mom says
such beautiful eyes it'd be a shame
if you were ever to lose one
she had tears in her eyes
after she said those nice thoughts

my mom and my dad discussed a long time
I could hear them through the door
it's not working
this place is too expensive
the roof is leaking even if it's a new house
our neighbours are awful
they look down on us
and Mary she acts like a dimwit
always hurting herself
you'd think she was running after trouble

each time my mother answered
it's OK! It's OK!
what counts is we all love each other
Mary will be more careful in the future
we could always move
to a different neighbourhood
where houses cost less
and neighbours are less snobby
mom was talking a mile a minute
she was afraid my father would cut her off

my father was answering
that it's all too complicated
that my mom just doesn't get it
that she is always crying
and it drives him mad

I could hear everything
but sometimes I'd miss some parts
especially when I'd hear the word carrion

then my father said
that in fact yes he would move
but just him without us
I thought not with the females of the house
but he didn't say it

my arm was completely numb
I got up
without disturbing my pets
they weren't sleeping neither
I put my ear up against the door
my dad was saying he wanted to go
mom was crying no
she didn't want him to leave
let go he said let go of me

he was shouting that we were poisoning his existence
that he just couldn't breathe anymore
that even the air in the house had become foul
and if things continued
he'd suffocate
my mom let out a laugh
she said if he was having trouble breathing
it was because of his nerves
my father was furious

so when I heard a loud bang
like a door slamming
or batting in the wind
cuz I heard it two three time in a row
and a chair toppling over
I got scared
maybe the television
was turned up too loud

and the yelling was coming from a TV show
then I heard the door to the garage slam
and the car starting up
in the garage
I could hear the motor running
I wondered what was going to happen next
but nothing happened at all

I decided to go see
my door didn't want to open
I concentrated
just try a little harder Mary
and it finally came unstuck
I put the guinea pig back in its cage
before opening my door all the way
I told Eugenya to stay on the bed
but the cat didn't listen
she left the room
at the same time as me

my mom was laying down
on the kitchen floor
I walked over
to my mother
she continued to lay there
not moving at all
on the black
and white tiles

a puddle of red
was spreading out
from under her

it's OK!
it's OK! I told myself
I could still hear the car engine
in the garage
but my father wasn't waiting
for anyone

it's OK!
Mom
I'll mend you
and
I sewed her back up
like I did with the cat
I placed my hands
on her tummy
I concentrated
really hard
like you have to concentrate
when you need to go poo
and nothin comes out

I went down to the garage
I tried to pull open the car door
it was locked from inside

I made a big effort
and the car unlocked
the buttons popped up
just like that
I turned the key and pulled it out
the car engine stopped running
my dad was fast asleep
so I let him keep sleeping
he was so exhausted
his shoulders were slumped
against the steering wheel

I placed the keys on his lap
I opened the garage door
by pressing on the big button
that way if he wanted to leave
he could go
there'd be nothing to stop him now

I went back to the kitchen
as my mom woke up
she asked me
what are you doing here
nothin
then go back to bed
did you hurt yourself Mom

mommy just fell
but didn't get injured
see she's fine
your mother had a fainting spell
that's all
that sometimes happens to mothers

she picked up the knife
from the floor
of the kitchen
she wiped it clean
she looked at it
like she was surprised
then she put the knife into the dishwasher
straightened one chair
then the other
she sat me down
then set it back at the table
she mopped up the blood
and led me all the way
back to my bed

she told the cat to get out
cuz he was up on my bed again
then she looked at the guinea pig
in its cage
and she said
I thought it had died

nope I said
look at the cat it's walking funny
you'd think he was drunk

alrighty now
into bed or your dad will get mad
when he comes back in
really that cat is acting so odd
like he doesn't know
which end is up

Eugenya will be fine Mom
a cat gots nine lives
she has only used up half of them
don't say gots Mary
Mom Mom
I don't feel too good
how many lives do I get

have you finished your homework

it doesn't matter
I think I won't go
to school tomorrow
tell the teacher that I am sick
that you told me to stay in bed

and why Miss Mary
should I tell her such lies

I can't take it any more
I've got cramps Mom
in my tummy

you're a bit young for that aren't you

I feel so totally
exhausted
I'm drained
it's as if I have no
life left inside me
I'm even having trouble
seeing you
Mom

Mary my sweet you're dead tired
it's time to get some rest my darling

Mom my homework
it's not finished

it'll do you good to sleep
tomorrow morning
we'll get up early
and we'll finish that homework
you'll see
I don't have any more strength
it's as if I gave all of it to you

my energy
Mom I won't even be able to walk
to get to school
tomorrow
for sure
it's
too far

come now Mary
don't think about that
my love
why are you getting up

I wanted to see what is happening
with Daddy

your father is sound asleep in the car
better that you not wake him up
he carries so much on his shoulders

daddy says the whole world
is always on his back

nighty night Mary
I want you to sleep
when your father comes in
I don't want you bothering him
Mom turned off the light

Mary
I love you

me too
Mom
I love you

go to sleep now
I want you to sleep
right now
it is nighttime

Mom I'm afraid that I'll die

come now Mary
no one dies
when they're eight years old

but Mom
I'm eight and a half

About the Translator

Growing up in Quebec, Ardeth Neale developed an early love for language and an understanding of its intimate relationship with literature and culture, which was further established though teaching, travel and translation. A graduate of Concordia University (B.Ed. TESL) and UQÀM (Cert. Adaptation Scolaire, Cert. Psychologie), Ardeth is presently enrolled in Concordia University's graduate diploma of Translation Program. Her recent literary work includes translation consultations for *The Girl Before, the Girl After* and editing of *The Sandcastle Diary* by the award-winning Quebec author Louis-Philippe Hébert. *Mary the Life Saver* is her first complete literary translation from French to English.

Other Books by the Author

IN ENGLISH

The Sandcastle Diary
Originally published in English, BookLand Press, 2014

The Girl Before, the Girl After
Translation of *Celle d'avant, celle d'après*
Translated by Jonathan Kaplansky, Quattro Books, 2014

IN FRENCH

Marie Réparatrice, Éditions de La Grenouillère, 2014
(Prix du Gouverneur Général, 2015)

Monsieur Blacquières, Éditions de La Grenouillère, 2014

La Cadillac du docteur Watson, Lévesque éditeur, 2013

Je suis un chien, Éditions de La Grenouillère, 2013

Celle d'avant, celle d'après, Lévesque éditeur, 2012

Vieillir, Les Herbes rouges, 2011
(Premier Prix du Festival de poésie de Montréal, 2012)

Les poèmes d'amour, Les Herbes rouges, 2010

Buddha Airlines, Les Herbes rouges, 2009

La chute de l'ange, Les Herbes rouges, 2009
(Prix Brigitte-Fontaine de l'Académie de la vie littéraire au XXIe siècle, 2009)

La bibliothèque de Sodome, Les Herbes rouges, 2008

Correspondance de guerre, Les Herbes rouges, 2008

Le livre des plages, Les Herbes rouges, 2007
(Grand Prix Québecor du Festival international de la poésie de Trois-Rivières, 2008)

IN SPANISH

Ya te dije por qué no queria envejecer?
Translation of *Vieillir, Volume 1*
Translated by Adrien Pelleumail, Editorial Leviatan, 2013

La mascara de la muerte
Translation of *Vieillir, Volume 2*
Translated by Adrien Pelleumail, Editorial Leviatan, 2013

IN RUSSIAN

Avialinii Bydda
Translation of *Buddha Airlines*
Translated by Alexander Orlov, Donomnilit, 2015

Konets sveta
Translation of *La fin du monde,* a poetry collection containing *Correspondance de guerre, La chute de l'ange* and *Vieillir.*
Translated by Alexander Orlov, Donomnilit, 2015

Poemy o lubvi
Translation of *Les poèmes d'amour*
Translated by Alexander Orlov, Donomnilit, 2014

Plyazhnye zapiski
Translation of *Le livre des plages*
Translated by Alexander Orlov, Donomnilit, 2014

IN AZERBAIJANI

Çimərlik Gündəliyi
Translation of *Le livre des plages*
Translated by Sabir Jabbarov, World Editions, 2015

IN ROMANIAN

Marie Vindecătoarea
Translation of *Marie Réparatrice.*
Translated by Flavia Cosma, Ars Longa, 2015